FULL SCORE

Jazz Recording Session Series
Jazz Combo: SEXTET

I0798700

Waiting

Idrees Sulieman & Kathe Laursen

Arranged by Don Sickler

Recorded by T.S. MONK
on TAKE ONE
Blue Note: CDP 7 99614

DON SICKLER, trumpet
BOBBY PORCELLI, alto sax
WILLIE WILLIAMS, tenor sax
RONNIE MATHEWS, piano
JAMES GENUS, bass
T.S. MONK, drums

Recorded on October 16, 1991

SEXTET INSTRUMENTATION

(recorded parts shown in bold type, alternate parts in light type)
1st part: **Trumpet**, Alto Sax
2nd part: **Alto Sax**, Tenor Sax
3rd part: **Tenor Sax**, Baritone Sax, Trombone
Rhythm Section: **Piano, Bass, Drums**, Guitar
FULL SCORE

SFM
A DON SICKLER PRODUCTION
SECOND FLOOR MUSIC

EXCLUSIVELY DISTRIBUTED BY
HAL•LEONARD® CORPORATION
7777 W. BLUEMOUND RD. P.O. BOX 13819 MILWAUKEE, WI 53213

HL00000503

Recorded by T.S. MONK on TAKE ONE (Blue Note CDP 7 99614 2)

FULL SCORE

WAITING

IDREES SULIEMAN
KÄTHE LAURSEN
Arranged by Don Sickler

Ballad (♩ = *ca.* 58)

Tpt
Alt
Ten
Pno
Bass
Dr
melody
fill
Gm7b5
C7(#11 #9)
C7(b9)
F7(13 b9)
B9
Bb9#5
Bb7(b9)
mp
mf
7
A1
Ebmaj7
Am7b5
Abm(maj7)
Abm6
Gm7
C7(b9)
11

Tpt
Alt
Ten
Pno
Bass
Dr
melody
mf
mp
Fm9
B9(13)
B♭9(13)
Gm7♭5
C7(♯11 ♯9)
C7(♭9)
15
melody
mp
mf
mp
mf
F7(13 ♭9)
B9
B♭9♯5
B♭7(♭9)
B♭m7(11)
E♭7
A7♯5
fill
19

* see footnote on page 7.

C
melody
Tpt
Alt
Ten
Pno
Bass
Dr
Ebmaj7
Am7b5
Abm(maj7)
Abm6
Gm7
C7(13 b9)
C7#5
mf
f
31
F7
Bb7
Ab7
G7#5
Db9
35

* The solo section ends 2 beats before Ⓕ on the recording, with everyone taking the 2-beat pick-up to Ⓒ *al fine.*
If the whole solo chorus is used, you can either take the 1st ending or 2nd ending.

RECORDED

TRUMPET (1st part)

Recorded by T.S. MONK on TAKE ONE (Blue Note CDP 7 99614 2)

WAITING

IDREES SULIEMAN
KÄTHE LAURSEN
Arranged by Don Sickler

Ballad (♩ = *ca.* 58)

engraved by Osho Endo

* The solo section ends 2 beats before (F) on the recording, with everyone taking the 2-beat pick-up to (C) *al fine.*
If the whole solo chorus is used, you can either take the 1st ending or 2nd ending.

Recorded by T.S. MONK on TAKE ONE (Blue Note CDP 7 99614 2)

ALTO SAX (1st part)

WAITING

IDREES SULIEMAN
KÄTHE LAURSEN
Arranged by Don Sickler

Ballad (♩ = *ca.* 58)

engraved by Osho Endo

* The solo section ends 2 beats before Ⓕ on the recording, with everyone taking the 2-beat pick-up to Ⓒ *al fine.*
If the whole solo chorus is used, you can either take the 1st ending or 2nd ending.

RECORDED

ALTO SAX (2nd part)

Recorded by T.S. MONK on TAKE ONE (Blue Note CDP 7 99614 2)

WAITING

IDREES SULIEMAN
KÄTHE LAURSEN
Arranged by Don Sickler

Ballad (♩ = *ca.* 58)

engraved by Osho Endo

* The solo section ends 2 beats before Ⓕ on the recording, with everyone taking the 2-beat pick-up to Ⓒ *al fine.*
If the whole solo chorus is used, you can either take the 1st ending or 2nd ending.

Recorded by T.S. MONK on TAKE ONE (Blue Note CDP 7 99614 2)

TENOR SAX (2nd part)

WAITING

IDREES SULIEMAN
KÄTHE LAURSEN
Arranged by Don Sickler

engraved by Osho Endo

* The solo section ends 2 beats before Ⓕ on the recording, with everyone taking the 2-beat pick-up to Ⓒ *al fine.*
If the whole solo chorus is used, you can either take the 1st ending or 2nd ending.

RECORDED

TENOR SAX (3rd part)

Recorded by T.S. MONK on TAKE ONE (Blue Note CDP 7 99614 2)

WAITING

IDREES SULIEMAN
KÄTHE LAURSEN
Arranged by Don Sickler

engraved by Osho Endo

* The solo section ends 2 beats before (F) on the recording, with everyone taking the 2-beat pick-up to (C) *al fine.*
If the whole solo chorus is used, you can either take the 1st ending or 2nd ending.

Recorded by T.S. MONK on TAKE ONE (Blue Note CDP 7 99614 2)

BARITONE (3rd part)

WAITING

IDREES SULIEMAN
KÄTHE LAURSEN
Arranged by Don Sickler

Ballad (♩ = *ca.* 58)

engraved by Osho Endo

* The solo section ends 2 beats before (F) on the recording, with everyone taking the 2-beat pick-up to (C) *al fine.*
If the whole solo chorus is used, you can either take the 1st ending or 2nd ending.

Recorded by T.S. MONK on TAKE ONE (Blue Note CDP 7 99614 2)

TROMBONE (3rd part)

WAITING

IDREES SULIEMAN
KÄTHE LAURSEN
Arranged by Don Sickler

engraved by Osho Endo

* The solo section ends 2 beats before (F) on the recording, with everyone taking the 2-beat pick-up to (C) *al fine.*
If the whole solo chorus is used, you can either take the 1st ending or 2nd ending.

RECORDED

PIANO

Recorded by T.S. MONK on TAKE ONE (Blue Note CDP 7 99614 2)

WAITING

IDREES SULIEMAN
KÄTHE LAURSEN
Arranged by Don Sickler

Ballad (♩ = *ca.* 58)

engraved by Osho Endo

* The solo section ends 2 beats before (F) on the recording, with everyone taking the 2-beat pick-up to (C) *al fine.*
If the whole solo chorus is used, you can either take the 1st ending or 2nd ending.

RECORDED

BASS

Recorded by T.S. MONK on TAKE ONE (Blue Note CDP 7 99614 2)

WAITING

IDREES SULIEMAN
KÄTHE LAURSEN
Arranged by Don Sickler

Ballad (♩ = *ca.* 58)

engraved by Osho Endo

* The solo section ends 2 beats before (F) on the recording, with everyone taking the 2-beat pick-up to (C) *al fine*.
If the whole solo chorus is used, you can either take the 1st ending or 2nd ending.

RECORDED

DRUMS

Recorded by T.S. MONK on TAKE ONE (Blue Note CDP 7 99614 2)

WAITING

IDREES SULIEMAN
KÄTHE LAURSEN
Arranged by Don Sickler

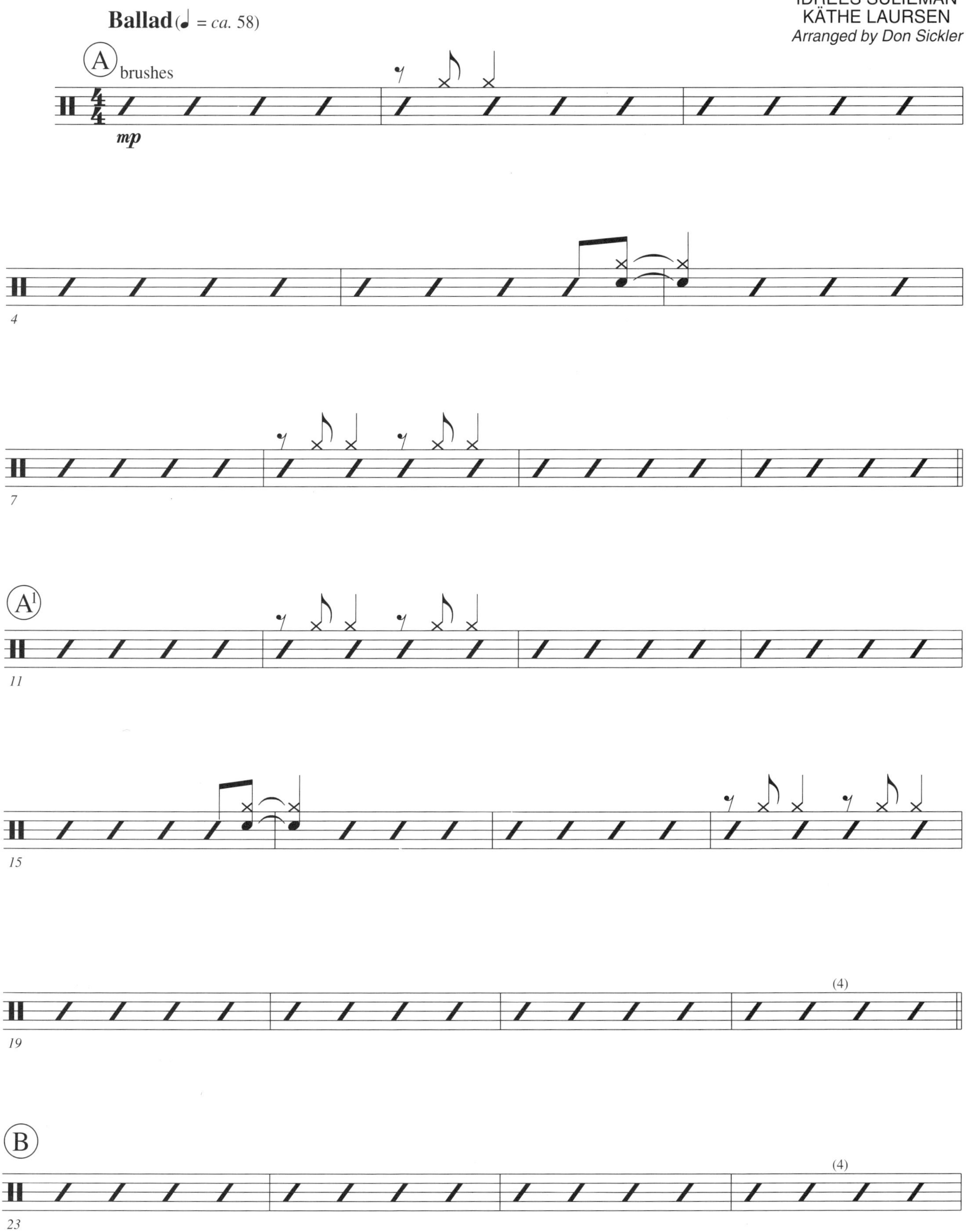

engraved by Osho Endo

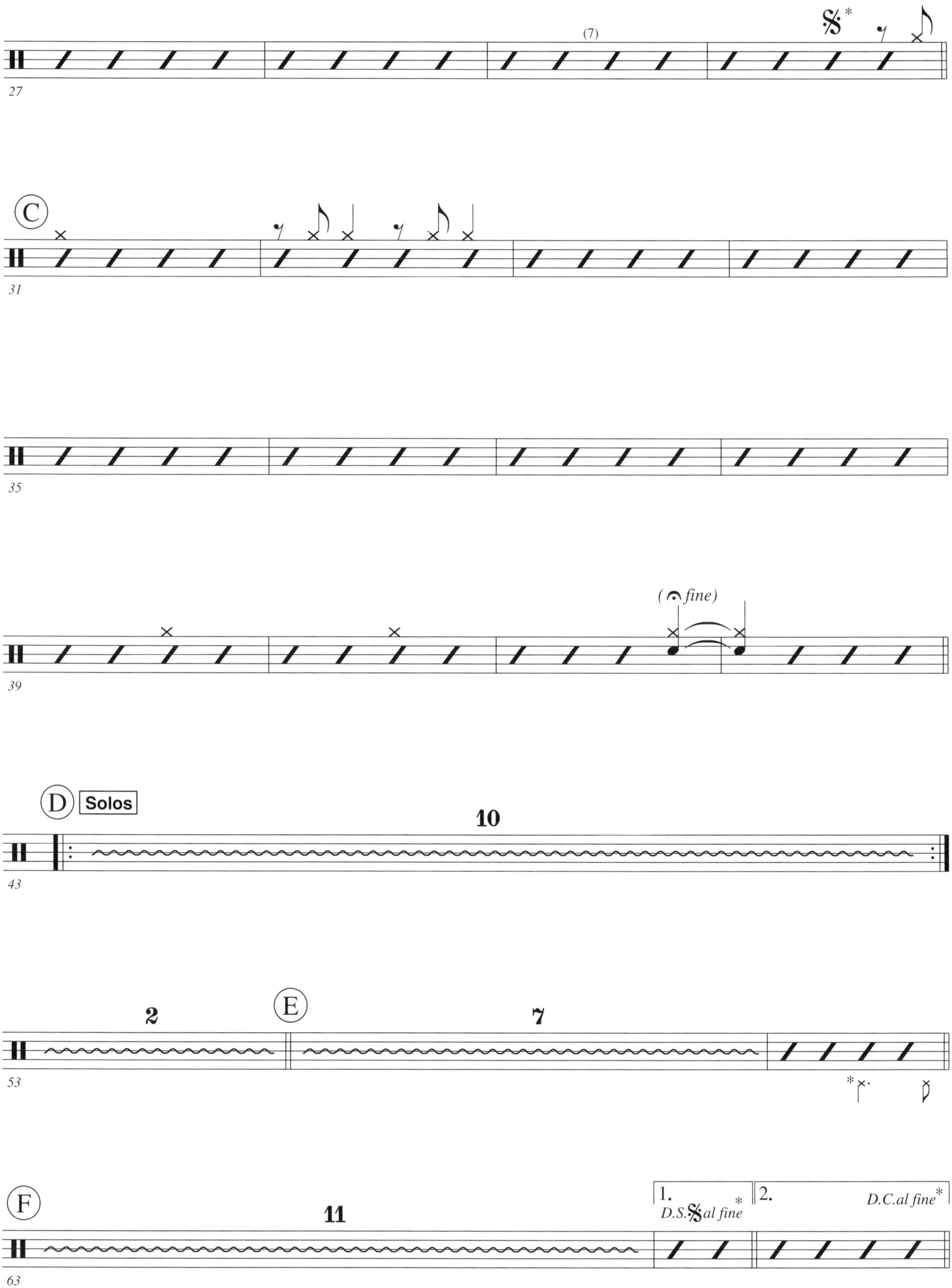

* The solo section ends 2 beats before (F) on the recording, with everyone taking the 2-beat pick-up to (C) *al fine*.
If the whole solo chorus is used, you can either take the 1st ending or 2nd ending.

Recorded by T.S. MONK on TAKE ONE (Blue Note CDP 7 99614 2)

GUITAR (rhythm section)

WAITING

IDREES SULIEMAN
KÄTHE LAURSEN
Arranged by Don Sickler

Ballad (♩ = ca. 58)

engraved by Osho Endo

* The solo section ends 2 beats before Ⓕ on the recording, with everyone taking the 2-beat pick-up to Ⓒ *al fine.* If the whole solo chorus is used, you can either take the 1st ending or 2nd ending.